FROM BLOSSOMS

Li-Young Lee was born in 1957 in Jakarta, Indonesia, of Chinese parents. His great-grandfather, Yuan Shikai, was China's first republican president (1912-16). His father, Lee Kuo Yuan, a deeply religious Christian physician, was personal secretary to Communist leader Mao Tse-tung. After they fell out, Lee's father escaped to Indonesia, where he helped found Gamaliel University, but was later imprisoned for 19 months in Sukarno's jails and in a leper colony, before he managed to escape and take his family out of the country. After a five-year trek through Hong Kong, Macau and Japan, they settled in the United States in 1964, where Lee's father became a Presbyterian minister. Assisting his father on preaching trips in Pennsylvania was another of Li-Young Lee's formative experiences.

Li-Young Lee has published five collections in the States: including *Rose* (1986), winner of the Delmore Schwartz Memorial Award; *The City in Which I Love You* (1991), the 1990 Lamont Poetry Selection; and *Book of My Nights* (2001), as well as a memoir, *The Winged Seed: A Remembrance* (1995), which received an American Book Award from the Before Columbus Foundation. His first British publication, *From Blossoms: Selected Poems* (Bloodaxe Books, 2007), draws on all four of these books. He has since published two other collections in the US, *Behind My Eyes* (2008) and *The Undressing* (2018). He lives in Chicago, Illinois.

LI-YOUNG LEE

From Blossoms

SELECTED POEMS

Copyright © Li-Young Lee 1986, 1990, 1995, 2001, 2007

ISBN: 978 1 85224 698 3

First published 2007 by
Bloodaxe Books Ltd,
Eastburn,
South Park,
Hexham,
Northumberland NE46 1BS.

www.bloodaxebooks.com
For further information about Bloodaxe titles
please visit our website and join our mailing list
or write to the above address for a catalogue.

LEGAL NOTICE
All rights reserved. No part of this book may be
reproduced, stored in a retrieval system, or
transmitted in any form, or by any means, electronic,
mechanical, photocopying, recording or otherwise,
without prior written permission from Bloodaxe Books Ltd.

Li-Young Lee has asserted his right under
Section 77 of the Copyright, Designs and Patents Act 1988
to be identified as the author of this work.

Cover design: Neil Astley & Pamela Robertson-Pearce.

Digital reprint of the 2007 Bloodaxe Books edition.

ACKNOWLEDGEMENTS

All the poems in this selection are drawn from Li-Young Lee's three collections, published in the USA by BOA Editions: *Rose* (1986), *The City in Which I Love You* (1990) and *Book of My Nights* (2001). Five poems appear in versions later than those published in *Book of My Nights*: 'Where Art Thou?' (previously titled 'Discrepancies, Happy and Sad'), 'Our River Now', 'In the Beginning', 'Fill and Fall' and 'Restless'. The prose extracts are all from *The Winged Seed* (Simon & Schuster, 1995).

For permission to reprint any of the poetry and prose by Li-Young Lee in this book, please contact: BOA Editions, 250 North Goodman Street, Suite 306, Rochester, NY 14607, USA.

The foreword by Xiaojing Zhou is adapted from an essay first published in *The Heath Anthology of American Literature*, 5th edition, vol. E (Houghton Mifflin, 2005), by kind permission of the author.

CONTENTS

9   *Foreword* by XIAOJING ZHOU

from THE WINGED SEED: A REMEMBRANCE (1995)
- 13   *Six extracts*

from ROSE (1986)
- 34   Epistle
- 36   The Gift
- 38   Persimmons
- 41   The Weight of Sweetness
- 42   From Blossoms
- 43   Dreaming of Hair
- 46   Early in the Morning
- 47   Irises
- 48   Eating Alone
- 49   Always a Rose
- 57   Eating Together
- 58   I Ask My Mother to Sing
- 59   Mnemonic
- 60   Between Seasons
- 61   Visions and Interpretations

from THE CITY IN WHICH I LOVE YOU (1990)
- 65   Furious Versions
- 79   The Interrogation
- 81   This Hour and What Is Dead
- 83   This Room and Everything In It
- 85   The City in Which I Love You
- 91   A Story
- 92   Goodnight
- 94   You Must Sing
- 95   Here I Am

from **BOOK OF MY NIGHTS** (2001)

   99   Pillow
100   A Table in the Wilderness
102   Hurry toward Beginning
104   Little Round
105   Where Art Thou?
107   My Father's House
110   The Moon from Any Window
112   Our River Now
113   The Bridge
114   Words for Worry
116   Little Father
117   Build by Flying
118   In the Beginning
119   The Hammock
120   The Eternal Son
122   Fill and Fall
124   Dwelling
125   Restless
127   Out of Hiding

FOREWORD

Li-Young Lee has been praised for his passionate poetry and its deceptively simple style. His poems are unique in their emotional intensity and metaphysical abstraction, particularly at a time when many contemporary American poets are breaking away from the "lyric I" in order to articulate an unstable and plural "I".

Lee's three prize-winning books, *Rose* (1986), *The City in Which I Love You* (1990), and *The Winged Seed: A Remembrance* (1995), share recurrent themes of love, exile, and mortality. Haunted by memories, Lee's poems are exploratory, showing a relentless search for understanding and for the right language to give form to what is invisible and evanescent. He once said, 'When I write, I'm trying to make that which is visible – this face, this body, this person – invisible, and at the same time, make what is invisible – that which exists at the level of pure being – completely visible.' Critics who celebrate the disappearance of the "lyric I" from postmodern poetry as the only possible way of opening the poetic to the historical and political might take issue with Lee's poetics. Yet for minority American poets like Lee to explore the interior and the abstract may not be as escapist or politically inconsequential as some critics might think.

Lee was born in 1957 in Indonesia of Chinese parents. His mother, a granddaughter of Yuan Shi-kai, China's first president (1912–16), married the son of a gangster and an entrepreneur. His parents' marriage in Communist China was much frowned upon, and they eventually fled to Indonesia, where Lee's father taught medicine and philosophy at Gamliel University in Jakarta.

In 1959, when Sukarno launched a violent ethnic purge of the Chinese, Lee's father was incarcerated for his interest in Western culture and ideas; he loved Shakespeare, opera, and Kierkegaard, and he taught the King James version of the Bible. After nineteen months of imprisonment, he escaped; with his family, he traveled to Macao, Japan, and Singapore before settling in Hong Kong, where he became a revered evangelist minister.

In 1964, the family emigrated to the United States. Lee's father studied at the Pittsburgh Theological Seminary and later became a Presbyterian minister.

Lee went to the University of Pittsburgh, where he took Gerald Stern's poetry writing class and earned his B.A. in 1979; he continued to study creative writing at the University of Arizona and the State University of New York at Brockport. He lives in Chicago with his wife and their two sons.

Lee's father and his family's experience of exile have had a significant impact on Lee's poetry. As a child, he learned to recite Chinese poems from the Tang dynasty (618–907) and was often enchanted by his father's poetic preaching and reading of the Psalms. Many of his poems recall his father, who is portrayed as strict and tender, powerful and vulnerable, godlike and human.

Breaking away from linear, rhetorical structure, Lee's poems unfold and expand from a central image, which holds together the discontinuous narratives and fragmentary scenes. Similar to the functions of imagery in classical Chinese poetry, his composition method gives him greater freedom in making leaps from narrative to lyricism and from the concrete to the abstract. Lee's poems bring together Eastern and Western ideas and traditions. Among the literary influences that Lee has acknowledged are the biblical Song of Songs, Gerald Stern's *Lucky Life*, Kierkegaard's *Fear and Trembling*, Meister Eckhart's sermons, and Rainer Maria Rilke's 'Duino Elegies'. The spiritual and emotional experience of the poems is accompanied by a down-to-earth sensualness that Lee says 'comes from my obsession with the body, man-body, earth-body, woman-body, father-body, mother-body, mind-body (for I experience the mind as another body) and the poem body'. This vision may suggest the influence of Whitman, but it is also rooted in Daoism. Lee is familiar with Daoist texts and admires Lao Zi, Lie Zi, and Zhuang Zi, whose sense of wonder and mystery and whose paradoxical and skeptical characteristics are evident in Lee's poems and prose-poem memoir.

XIAOJING ZHOU

FROM BLOSSOMS

from
THE WINGED SEED:
A REMEMBRANCE
(1995)

I remember, as long as I knew him, my father carried at all times in his right suit-pocket a scarce handful of seeds. *Remembrance*, was his sole answer when I asked him why. He was pithy. He slept with his head on a stone wrapped in a piece of white linen I washed once a week. Up until I was nine years old, I napped with him, making myself as small as possible so as not to wake him. I remember how, when he turned over in bed, I made room, wedging myself against the wall, my left arm under my head for a pillow, my legs numb. I lay very quietly while he snored. I lay wide awake against his flesh while he slept with his head on the stone wrapped in the cloth which smelled of his hair, a rich oil. When he died, the stone kept a faintest impression that fit the shape of his head. My mother carried it out, and left it under one of the thirty-six pines that enclosed two sides of the property on which our house stood, the third side the fence where the morning glory climbed. Some days the depression in my father's pillow must fill with rain, just enough to give a cardinal a drink. Or maybe somebody has found it by now, has used it as part of a wall, where it fits to another stone shaped like a man's skull. We burned most everything else before selling the house and moving. Out of the heap of his papers, notebooks, manuscripts, photographs, and letters, my sister Fei, almost obligingly, chose one scrapbook of newspaper clippings to keep, which none of us ever looked at after we left Pennsylvania. Everything else we fed to a roaring fire we'd made in the backyard between two apple trees. While we all stood about the fire, which we kept alive two days and two nights without sleeping, one hot mote shot out and creased my youngest brother's thigh, burning through the cloth of his pants and several layers of skin. His leg owns the scar to this day.

I never asked my father in remembrance of what he kept those seeds. I knew better than to press him when I was a boy. Now I'm a man, and he is dead, and I feel a strange shame that I don't know what happened to those seeds. Did we bury them with him? Is morning glory breaking his pewter casket's tight lip this second? Is morning glory blooming on a cemetery hill in Pennsylvania? Didn't I one day kneel in the mud and snow, halfway up a hillside, halfway to my father's grave, and hold my wrist to an icy cataract, and see the shriveled vine and the gold seed pods?

❧

What did my father mean when he said *Remembrance*? I remember I was born in the City of Victory on a street called Jilan Industri, where each morning the man selling sticky rice cakes goes by pushing his cart, his little steamer whistling, and by noon the lychee man passes, his head in a rag, bundles of the fruit strung on the pole slung on his neck, while at his waist, at the end of a string, a little brass bell shivers into a fine and steady seizure. I remember I was named twice, once at my birth, and once again after my father, in his prison cell, dreamed each night the same dream, in which the sun appeared to him as a blazing house, wherein dwelt a seed, black, new, dimly human. And so one morning, at a white metal table in the visiting yard, he and my mother decided my name, which, said one way, indicates the builded light of the pearl, and said another, the sun.

It was 1959, the year of the pig, eighteen months after I was born, that my father was arrested by the military police working under President Sukarno, because of things he'd been saying to a handful of men and women who came down every evening to the banks of the Solo River to wash their rice, or beat their clothes clean on the stones, or shit behind the makeshift rattan screens. He'd been warned several times before his arrest that what he talked about those evenings, sitting beside the Solo, might be considered seditious. When he didn't stop, the Indonesian War Administration accused him of being a spy, and threw him in prison for nineteen months. But what could a person say about night and seeds, for it was night and seeds my father talked about, that might so offend a military regime? What is a seed? My son's fourth-grade textbook says something about monocots and dicots. Is it monocot or dicot seeds dictators fear? What was so dangerous about the letters he wrote to my mother and had smuggled out of jail that she had to burn them immediately after she read them? What does a seed enclose that might be considered dangerous to anyone? What was it my father said, standing at evening by the Solo?

Did he say seed planted deep at one sill declares a new house at a further turn of the sun?

Did he say seed is good news, our waiting done?

Did he say seed is told, kept cold, scored with a pocket-knife, and then left out to die, in order to come into a further seed, speaking the father seed, leading to seed, if seed can be said to lead, a road we sow ahead of our arrival?

What did he say? Think.

Once upon a time, a seed went walking down a spiral stair, having gotten it in his head he wanted to become a rice. *When*, he wondered, *will I lie down a seed only, a lone stone, and wake up an assembly that feeds, a great rice?* He wanted to feed. *Seed dies*, he thought, *but rice never sleeps, rice is unvanquished.* So he went walking, and asking, *Are you my father?* and *Are you my mother?* of a door, a mirror, and a kitchen knife. The door pinched him, the mirror declared nothing the seed recognised, and the kitchen knife said, *Good night.*

What? asked the seed. *Did you say something?*

Toll, whispered the knife.

Toll? asked the seed.

Pay the toll. You must reckon with your passage.

I have no money, said the seed.

Then I kill you now, whispered the knife. The seed shuddered, and a very thin layer of skin sloughed off.

Wait, he said, *I can give you a riddle.*

A riddle? asked the blade.

I'm good at riddling. I'm a seed.

The blade considered. *All right*, he said, *but I'm not bad at riddling myself. So tell a riddle I can't unriddle, or you don't pass. No, tell me three.*

The seed thought hard. His first riddle was this:

What an unlikely hand, the wing. What weird feet, claws. What fine math, a nest. What a strange bird, the ear that speaks a flower. It's nearly an open eye. How dark the ore that lies awake all night. And what an unlikely miner, the heart who comes, a hand his only lamp. And what an odd compass, a pebble in a shoe, the heel the only comfort. And what a strange mountain, a seed. What an unlikely kingdom. How narrow a house it keeps. So little shelters us. How still the next world lies inside it.

That's easy, whispered the knife, scraping himself against a whetstone. *The answer is: pilgrim. You're down to two.*

The seed thought harder. His second riddle was this:

My foot, a balding paw, would like to be a hand, recalls too well the wolf it is, would like to play a piano, compose a sonata, knot a tie, don a uniform of thirty buttons. The boot is what it dreams. It loves the heel, adores the glove. My wolf despises what it wants to be, my hand. It steps on the hand, would extinguish the seed buried in the valley of the thumb and index, in the girlish wrist, the ticklish palm, for the hand claps and the wolf dances, the fingers count and he leads the path to water, the map drawn on the foot's own ticklish belly, which a man reads by a hand that touches, that loves the wolf that bites.

The knife yawned. *You better do better than that. You'll be dead sooner than you think. The answer is: siblings.*

The seed began to worry. What was he to do? Those were two of his best riddles, and the knife unriddled them without breaking a sweat on his gleaming forehead. Then he told another:

A woman draws twelve animals on the wall. A man counts the eyes and feet and comes up odd. The window common to them says *Today*, and today a man will come. A man but not a man, riding but not sitting, standing but not leaning on a ladder, bone. A man ringing, rung with the twelve secret hips of honey, a signal odor of chrysanthemums, the recipe for snow, and the permanent address of the rose. His kisses seal the crossbar under which the two come and go: once to fetch the water and bring it back, once to fetch the children and bring them home, and one last time to hear the folded note a bird left at the end of their human year, all fire.

The knife was stumped. He suspected a trick. *A trick*, he mumbled, *a trick. You're tricking me.*

No, said the seed. *It's a riddle, and a good one. Now hear another*. With confidence renewed the seed told an other:

The woman I love gives half her face to the night. The other half she offers to me and one long window that stands at the end of the longest hall of the house I abandoned in a field of dandelion one day while the seed was blowing and the townspeople pulled down the bell-house and the one-eyed bell, and put up a blind clocktower. Is it my mother's house? Is it my father's? From where come the voices of the children?

The woman I love gives half her face to the night, in which she pauses on a stair to hear the water falling down for miles, and coming from unroofed leagues, and cold, so cold it numbs her mouth and wakes a seed, kissed into flowering.

The knife was almost wild with rage. *This better not be a trick*, he whispered.

Do you need more time? asked the seed, *or shall I assume I've told two which are beyond you? Let me tell my third, then I'll be on my way.* The seed began.

My right hand writes my letters, my left hand smuggles a seed into the ground. My hungry hand blesses. My fat hand reprimands. But my fat worm gets hungry, and though my woman lies unguarded, I ask where's the door? Where the morning glory closes at evening. Which is past the great meadows of cotton gins, and steel mills abandoned to clover and the honeybee, in whose antennae hums a spiral code and bright arithmetic.

Where the morning glory closes at evening, an unfinished house stands. And the house accomplished. There a bird flits between opposite sills, a facing ledge and my own, which I can't see, many dark elbows down and hidden by an eave.

Opposite houses and the one I inhabit is twice–hidden, by light all day, by nearness the long night, when I lean on a jamb to hear a bird call from its unseen sleep. Opposite calls, and one is heard, the one without a destiny, untroubled by the color of your hair, unencumbered of any wish, while unheard goes the very shape of longing, the sum of an unencompassable face, the call without seam or margin, and we face it.

So tell the man whose head is bowed, who's waiting to hear from me, if he looks up he'll see the guests are leaving the feast. Tell him while his one hand inches along the frayed margin of his father's cloth his mother mends, the other hand falls to the threshing floor to lie, blind among the blind grain. But don't tell him my name.

And he who loved me once, who has forgotten me, all of me fallen from him like scales or old thorns, making his journey lighter, tell him his shadow of discarded leagues arrives before him everywhere he goes. And she who had forgotten me, who thinks of me tonight, doubling me by patiently not finding me under her cooking spoon, in either furrow between her eyes, tell her I'm close, the insect counting in her unguarded wrist.

But don't tell either of them my name.

And the boy who would make my picture with his pencil, who draws the lines over and over, multiplying me, his drawing hand growing sore, his paper beginning to tear, tell that one who darkens me, and darkens me, and darkens me, don't cry! The path relinquished finds its way is home by a star's influence. Lift your face from your hands, tell him, and set it toward an indoor sea. See? It becomes what it faces. And the hands, the hands hang. Leave them. Tell him they'll find water. But don't tell him my name.

It's nice riddling with you, but I really must go now. I'm going to be a rice. Then he started walking away, but as he turned to go, the knife, incensed at having been bested, suspicious at having been duped, flew down from the cutting-board on which he'd been standing, and struck the seed, killing him on the spot.

But what is a seed? Is it the apple? Is it a Kingdom? To hold a seed, weightless, in the palm of your hand, is to think, *Soon.* If it is a morning glory seed, you hold both the flower and where the flower closes at evening, where another country begins, and double doors open toward us, the seam of their parting widening to vanquish utter margins unto the first day: Noon, a woman is dressing for our journey together, combing her hair opposite the direction of our arrival. Her name appears in ledgers of ships whose masts have long passed out of view, dispelling any rumor of a horizon or setting sun. And soon, the sun, that bell, struck some million years ago, will tell the note it meant. Soon, a seed will wake, who lay all night along a ledge. Meanwhile, I cradle in my hand this odorless seed like one dead, like one who recalls nothing of his actions or inactions, one who bears inside now only a remembered shapeliness of certain desires and needs, no longer recognisable as desire or need, but things more elemental, akin to oceans, sandstorms, and the yearning wings reveal by their action in time. I remember the back gate where I planted morning glory seven years ago. Walking there last fall, I noticed that the vine had dropped all its flowers. But the leaves were intact; green, heart-shaped, they hid the pods that kept the seeds.

A morning glory's seedpods took like miniature sultans' turbans and each is as big as a good-size drop of blood. Shaking them a little, the rattling made me think that each might hold inside it a meticulous clock Breaking them open, I saw they were merely the gold husk to the blacker thoughts, the seeds! Thought is black! Why does the morning glory have no fruit? What does the flower signal? Each year I must wait past the glory's green polyp, past the bruise-colored bud, and later than the lavender flower, in order to break into the gold pods, pop them between my fingers, and scatter black, news-bearing seeds in a glass dish.

I remember my father's sermon on the seed, which he told by candlelight, in the church basement in Pennsylvania. It was during the blizzard of 1975. The Women's Auxiliary sat in a circle around him, sewing blankets. He leaned across a table and said that the hour had come for us to put an ear to the seed, to hear the lightning scratched there, late news of our human spring. Or was that his sermon on the spring? From my father's sermon on the trees, I remember only the sound of trees. From things he said on the falling leaves, I recall a rake left lying in the apple orchard. From what he told about the seven boats, all I have are ten broken stairs darkening to the sea. What was it he said about the seed? Only the seed that hoarded winter to its heart...? Only the water broken into by winter could... No. That was his sermon on winter. On that topic he had a lot to say; so much, in fact, that he devoted a month of Sundays to it, though I remember only his notion that there were not many winters in a life, but only one, a fathering winter, a paternal January and eternal season. That, he claimed, is the winter we have to outwinter, crucial season of death. In the face of death's winter, it's best to keep a wintering heart, detached to its depths, the wider scope of indifference. That was his January message, told with alarm in his otherwise even voice, like a warning I keep in my head these days when I am the exact age he was when I was born. His symbol for attachment was the proverbial house built on sand. Disengagement turns the ground solid, was what he tried to tell me. I regarded his words as the natural claim of a man who'd been forced to disengage over and over, having at eight years old lost a sister to rabies, at twelve the nanny who helped birth him and even fed him her milk, at sixteen a mother to murder, at twenty-five a first son to China, and at thirty a second to meningitis. So if he thought he was warning me, or anyone else, I think he was talking to himself those afternoons. Those afternoons in winter all become one winter afternoon, a room of light scarcely furnished with a ladder-backed chair; a cold, bright, enclosed porch where dry, brittle ivy hung like small bells from stone pots and my father stood talking, while I wrote down what he said. For I was my father's secretary from the time my writing was legible to him, around the age of fourteen. I wrote what my father thought out loud each Friday after school, helped him memorise it all day Saturday, and knew if he spoke or misspoke Sunday morning, when he opened his mouth for the sermon.

He began reciting on Saturdays when the sun was slightly past its zenith, yet bright in the highest ice-tipped branches of all four black trees outside the manse windows. The tree trunks were cast into shade, as half the house was by afternoon, from which depths a child's voice, my brother's, could be heard. He was reading out loud the stories from that great book our father made us read each day and my brother read all day Saturday. I could hear my brother's bored monotone coming from his shut room, while I listened to my father recite, and I read along in silence the typed draft of his previous day's thinking, I wished I could be reading the book my brother was reading.

My father was not among us, for he'd been arrested months ago by the military police, and was now in prison awaiting trial. High on a wall was the poster of the man who'd had him arrested: Sukarno, president of the Republic of Indonesia. His huge head set on a thick neck, he seemed to gaze over the commotion of the market, over the roofs of stalls and the heads of shoppers, the tables of meats, and fruits, and cloths, and vegetables, and assorted musical instruments and Moslem paraphernalia, over the traffic of the daily, over the trees, over the River Solo, over the tumult of the present into some other clarity. For he had a look about him of someone whose attention was wholly trained upon a great immanence. The artist of the poster must have been looking up at him when the portrait was made, for the contour of the head with a fez on it, and the massive, medal-bedecked shoulders, resembled nothing so much as an image hewn from a cliff.

While his face was everywhere, our father, on the other hand, was hidden from us, a prisoner in the ruler's palace, so we believed. The palace was surrounded by armored cars, jeeps, and khaki-uniformed, belt-strapped men, wearing buttons and medals and guns. And then, just as suddenly, Fei gasped, *It's Ba! Where?* our mother asked, startled. *It's Ba!* Fei said again, pointing to the poster. And when our mother saw that Fei was pointing at the picture of Sukarno, she broke into tears. We pleaded, *Don't cry, Mu, it's Ba*, while she shook her head, explaining that, no, it wasn't our father. *Have you forgotten what your father looks like?* she asked.

The fact is, by that time, our father seemed a virtual stranger to us, and the hours we spent waiting for him seemed endless. And while our mother's absence from us as she spent all her days at the prison became an emptiness around which our activities circled, it only punctuated that greater absence we called Ba, our father. Though our mother was often absent, Ba was The Absent One. He grew immense as our mother's days and thoughts revolved around his not being there. And though we daily hoped for his release, his absence had begun to feel like a permanence we simply lived with, never doubting it, reliable as gravity, or True North. It became our very world, and as a world, he became less keenly felt, more and more assumed, as though we'd always lived without him, as though he hadn't been taken from us only six months ago, but ages ago. Ba's absence receded from our daily thoughts into abstraction, even while we became its most intimate inhabitants. And this even though we prayed in front of his picture each night.

Each night, our mother repeated for us the story of our father: he was a prisoner, she would try to get him out, we had to pray. By that time, though, our praying had changed. Without our realising it, the subject of our prayers, Ba, had gradually become the object of our prayers as well, so that we were praying to him as well as for him. Each night, standing before his photograph, my brother Go and I on either side of our sister, Fei, we prayed, ending, *Dear Ba. Help Ba. We love Ba. Amen.* Judging by the way we prayed, it was up to Ba to get himself out of his absence and restore himself to us.

When my father preached between 1963 and 1964, on the island of Hong Kong, he drew crowds in such numbers that rows of folding chairs had to be set up in the very lobbies of the theaters where his revival meetings took place, while loudspeakers were set up outside, where throngs of sweating believers stood for hours in the sun, listening to him speak and pray.

Once, while my sister and I were buying sugarcane from our favorite street vendor, the afternoon suddenly filled with red and blue leaflets dropped from an airplane. My sister snatched one out of the air and the two of us looked at a picture of our father, under which was printed, in Chinese and English, the words *Your Friend*, and then the time and place of the next meeting of the Ling Liang Assembly and Ambassadors for Christ. I recognised the photograph as the same one my mother had taken of our father a little over a year ago on the boat from Indonesia to Hong Kong. His profile, taken by the camera from a lower angle, was backed by the sky and mast, perfect for the image of a helmsman or captain of souls. Only his family knew that when the photo was taken, we were on the way to a detention center. My father and his family were being shipped from one prison in Jakarta to another on some remote island, where, so we were told, we would be given a house and yard which we would not be permitted to leave. But on the way there, a former student of his from Gamaliel University pulled up alongside the ship with a smaller boat, so my parents assembled us in the night, and one stood above the other and handed to the one below, by hoisting over a railing, one by one, each of their five children. The two boats, big and small, rocked unevenly, the gap between them closing and widening, yet less dangerous than a guard asleep somewhere, or else awake but turned away to earn my father's bribe. By the next morning we were in the home of a congregation member of the Ling Liang Assembly. It was during one of the evening revival meetings, when members from the congregation gave personal testimonies of the working hand of God, that my father, convinced we had escaped harm due to some miracle and for some higher purpose, recounted the horrors of the last three years fleeing Sukarno and our rescue. Within a year of that testimony, he was performing mass baptisms in the ocean at night. Hundreds gathered once a month on the beach to watch my father take off his silk suit jacket, his narrow leather shoes and silk socks, roll up his sleeves and wade out into the dark water, from where we could hear him beckoning, *Come! Come to me, come farther, don't be afraid.* And one by one he embraced them and plunged them backward into the surf.

When Ba was a boy, he lived in an old, falling-down, two-story house that must have once been beautiful with its carved balustrades, and red tile roof, the edges of the flared eaves encrusted with ceramic figures. By the time he was born, though, the place, long neglected, was nothing but a creaky-staired hull of flaking paint and broken trim, with grass and little trees sprouting in the cracked brick courtyard, and so many empty rooms he couldn't imagine what they were for, and none of them heated in winter. He lived with his mother, a sister, and a brother in a few rooms at the front of the building, while the rooms at the back stood abandoned. All of them but two, in which his grandmother and her brother lived, the old woman seldom showing her face for fear of seeing her son, and the old man confined by locks and chains. Ba's father lived with them a few days a week in that house in the countryside outside Peking and kept an apartment in the city, where he did most of his work.

His family had been wealthy for a long time, establishing their money in the fishing industry, but most of the money had long been squandered and badly invested when Ba's father was old enough to wish it weren't so. He ended up with only the house when his father died. His mother was left owning a match factory which she had no idea how to run, and which Ba's father would inherit when she died. Ba's father made his living traveling as a broker in antiques and precious stones. By guile, charm, and good looks, and the knack for singling out suckers and first-time buyers and sellers, he not only swindled amazing sums of money but ended up amassing a decent collection of antiques.

Of course, his reputation spread, and he could not count on working in the same area for very long. So he traveled, and in the meantime, he bought a car and chauffeur, tailored European suits and hats, and visited America and Indonesia two or three times. But even as his family watched him get richer, not much changed for them, though they listened to his plans and promises to change their wretched lives. The house remained derelict, unheated in fall and winter. The ceilings leaked during rain. He was gone most of the time and never left them food or money.

I don't know how he thought we were surviving, Ba told me, as I bathed him one day, the body I became custodian to when I turned eighteen, after his fourth heart attack. Once a week I lifted Ba from his dying-bed, stripped him, and put him in the water.

My grandmother supported us with the diminishing profits from the factory. In fact, when my father was gone, we got to eat, while when he was home we starved. For he considered our eating a lack of filial piety. We were to defer to him in everything. I listened, I soaped his bony shoulders and his skinny neck where the collarbones jutted hugely their knuckles. I lifted his arm and soaped its pale, flaccid length, and then the ribs, where R feasted. *And since any food put in our mouths was looked upon as food taken out of his, our times with him resembled a strange kind of playacting. After the maid had set the food on the table, plates and plates of deliciously prepared meats and vegetables, my father would smile and ask, his voice full of merriment, 'Shall we eat?' and we had to answer, 'No thank I you, Father, we've eaten.' Then he would act genuinely surprised, even though it was the same routine each time, and he'd ask, 'Eaten? Are you sure? Why not have a bite with your father?' At which we were to insist, 'No thank you, Father. We're too full, but you should go ahead and enjoy yourself.'*

The shoulder-blades, as I glided my hand over them, seemed like hinges where old wings might have once been jointed. I noticed again the bloated feet and the missing toenails. I recalled his telling me when I was a boy how he'd lost his toenails in prison, but that was another story. Here, my father was telling me how his father ate with relish while his family watched, starved and yearning for just one taste of anything on the table. And while he ate, he thanked out loud the gods for the blessing of children with such a deep sense of honor and love for the patriarch. My father's mother, who also participated in the farce, sat opposite her husband at the long table, smiling, starving, and agreeing aloud with him. The leftovers, as a rule, were thrown in the garbage, which the patriarch inspected himself to make sure, he claimed, that none of his beloved family should eat food that had been left out too long. So they were happy to see him go on his business trips. When he stayed at home longer than three days they barely survived. For only in secret did they live on the food the grandmother bought and her maid prepared. Once, when Ba's father found out that his wife and children were eating, he beat them all with a stick, screaming like a madman, *Do I not provide for you that you should eat from another's kindness?* while the woman and the children begged his forgiveness and apologised over and over.

Even his own mother was afraid of him. And when she found out that he was planning to murder her in order to speed his inheriting the match factory, she signed the whole thing over to him on the spot. He turned right around and sold it for a huge profit, and then the family moved to Tientsin, where no one had heard of him, for his name had become, as they say, like the smell of dog shit on your shoes.

from
ROSE
(1986)

Epistle

Of wisdom, splendid columns of light
waking sweet foreheads,
I know nothing

but what I've glimpsed in my most hopeful of daydreams.
Of a world without end,
amen,

I know nothing,
but what I sang of once with others,
all of us standing in the vaulted room.

But there is wisdom
in the hour in which a boy
sits in his room listening

to the sound of weeping
coming from some other room
of his father's house,

and that boy was me, and he
listened without understanding, and was soon frightened
by how the monotonous sobs resembled laughter.

All of this while noon became vast day,
while sunlight and the clock
gave birth to melancholy,

before the days grew vacant,
the sun grew terrible, the clock stopped,
and melancholy gave up to grief.

All of this
in a dead hour of a dead day,
among doors closed for nap or prayer.

Who was weeping? Why?
Did the boy fall asleep?
Did he flee that house? Is he there now?

Before it all gets wiped away, let me say,
there is wisdom in the slender hour
which arrives between two shadows.

It is not heavenly and it is not sweet.
It is accompanied by steady human weeping,
and twin furrows between the brows,

but it is what I know,
and so am able to tell.

The Gift

To pull the metal splinter from my palm
my father recited a story in a low voice.
I watched his lovely face and not the blade.
Before the story ended, he'd removed
the iron sliver I thought I'd die from.

I can't remember the tale,
but hear his voice still, a well
of dark water, a prayer.
And I recall his hands,
two measures of tenderness
he laid against my face,
the flames of discipline
he raised above my head.

Had you entered that afternoon
you would have thought you saw a man
planting something in a boy's palm,
a silver tear, a tiny flame.
Had you followed that boy
you would have arrived here,
where I bend over my wife's right hand.

Look how I shave her thumbnail down
so carefully she feels no pain.
Watch as I lift the splinter out.
I was seven when my father
took my hand like this,

and I did not hold that shard
between my fingers and think,
Metal that will bury me,
christen it Little Assassin,
Ore Going Deep for My Heart.

And I did not lift up my wound and cry,
Death visited here!
I did what a child does
when he's given something to keep.
I kissed my father.

Persimmons

In sixth grade Mrs Walker
slapped the back of my head
and made me stand in the corner
for not knowing the difference
between *persimmon* and *precision*.
How to choose

persimmons. This is precision.
Ripe ones are soft and brown-spotted.
Sniff the bottoms. The sweet one
will be fragrant. How to eat:
put the knife away, lay down newspaper.
Peel the skin tenderly, not to tear the meat.
Chew the skin, suck it,
and swallow. Now, eat
the meat of the fruit,
so sweet,
all of it, to the heart.

Donna undresses, her stomach is white.
In the yard, dewy and shivering
with crickets, we lie naked,
face-up, face-down.
I teach her Chinese.
Crickets: *chiu chiu*. Dew: I've forgotten.
Naked: I've forgotten.
Ni, wo: you and me.
I part her legs,
remember to tell her
she is beautiful as the moon.

Other words
that got me into trouble were
fight and *fright*, *wren* and *yarn*.
Fight was what I did when I was frightened,
fright was what I felt when I was fighting.

Wrens are small, plain birds,
yarn is what one knits with.
Wrens are soft as yarn.
My mother made birds out of yarn.
I loved to watch her tie the stuff;
a bird, a rabbit, a wee man.

Mrs Walker brought a persimmon to class
and cut it up
so everyone could taste
a *Chinese apple*. Knowing
it wasn't ripe or sweet, I didn't eat
but watched the other faces.

My mother said every persimmon has a sun
inside, something golden, glowing,
warm as my face.

Once, in the cellar, I found two wrapped in newspaper,
forgotten and not yet ripe.
I took them and set both on my bedroom windowsill,
where each morning a cardinal
sang, *The sun, the sun.*

Finally understanding
he was going blind,
my father sat up all one night
waiting for a song, a ghost.
I gave him the persimmons,
swelled, heavy as sadness,
and sweet as love.

This year, in the muddy lighting
of my parents' cellar, I rummage, looking
for something I lost.
My father sits on the tired, wooden stairs,
black cane between his knees,
hand over hand, gripping the handle.

He's so happy that I've come home.
I ask how his eyes are, a stupid question.
All gone, he answers.

Under some blankets, I find a box.
Inside the box I find three scrolls.
I sit beside him and untie
three paintings by my father:
Hibiscus leaf and a white flower.
Two cats preening.
Two persimmons, so full they want to drop from the cloth.

He raises both hands to touch the cloth,
asks, *Which is this?*

This is persimmons, Father.

Oh, the feel of the wolftail on the silk,
the strength, the tense
precision in the wrist.
I painted them hundreds of times
eyes closed. These I painted blind.
Some things never leave a person:
scent of the hair of one you love,
the texture of persimmons,
in your palm, the ripe weight.

The Weight of Sweetness

No easy thing to bear, the weight of sweetness.

Song, wisdom, sadness, joy: sweetness
equals three of any of these gravities.

See a peach bend
the branch and strain the stem until
it snaps.
Hold the peach, try the weight, sweetness
and death so round and snug in your palm.
And, so, there is
the weight of memory:

Windblown, a rain-soaked
bough shakes, showering
the man and the boy.
They shiver in delight,
and the father lifts from his son's cheek
one green leaf
fallen like a kiss.

The good boy hugs a bag of peaches
his father has entrusted
to him.
Now he follows
his father, who carries a bagful in each arm.
See the look on the boy's face
as his father moves
faster and farther ahead, while his own steps
flag, and his arms grow weak, as he labors
under the weight
of peaches.

From Blossoms

From blossoms comes
this brown paper bag of peaches
we bought from the boy
at the bend in the road where we turned toward
signs painted *Peaches.*

From laden boughs, from hands,
from sweet fellowship in the bins,
comes nectar at the roadside, succulent
peaches we devour, dusty skin and all,
comes the familiar dust of summer, dust we eat.

O, to take what we love inside,
to carry within us an orchard, to eat
not only the skin, but the shade,
not only the sugar, but the days, to hold
the fruit in our hands, adore it, then bite into
the round jubilance of peach.

There are days we live
as if death were nowhere
in the background; from joy
to joy to joy, from wing to wing,
from blossom to blossom to
impossible blossom, to sweet impossible blossom.

Dreaming of Hair

Ivy ties the cellar door
in autumn, in summer morning glory
wraps the ribs of a mouse.
Love binds me to the one
whose hair I've found in my mouth,
whose sleeping head I kiss,
wondering is it death?
beauty?   this dark
star spreading in every direction from the crown of her head.

My love's hair is autumn hair, there
the sun ripens.
My fingers harvest the dark
vegetable of her body.
In the morning I remove it
from my tongue and
sleep again.

Hair spills
through my dream, sprouts
from my stomach, thickens my heart,
and tangles the brain. Hair ties the tongue dumb.
Hair ascends the tree
of my childhood – the willow
I climbed
one bare foot and hand at a time,
feeling the knuckles of the gnarled tree, hearing
my father plead from his window, *Don't fall!*

In my dream I fly
past summers and moths,
to the thistle
caught in my mother's hair, the purple one
I touched and bled for,
to myself at three, sleeping
beside her, waking with her hair in my mouth.

Along a slippery twine of her black hair
my mother ties *ko-tze* knots for me:
fish and lion heads, chrysanthemum buds, the heads
of Chinamen, black-haired and frowning.

Li-En, my brother, frowns when he sleeps.
I push back his hair, stroke his brow.
His hairline is our father's, three peaks pointing down.

What sprouts from the body
and touches the body?
What filters sunlight
and drinks moonlight?
Where have I misplaced my heart?
What stops wheels and great machines?
What tangles in the bough
and snaps the loom?

Out of the grave
my father's hair
bursts. A strand
pierces my left sole, shoots
up bone, past ribs,
to the broken heart it stitches,
then down,
swirling in the stomach, in the groin, and down,
through the right foot.

What binds me to this earth?
What remembers the dead
and grows toward them?

I'm tired of thinking.
I long to taste the world with a kiss.
I long to fly into hair with kisses and weeping,
remembering an afternoon
when, kissing my sleeping father, I saw for the first time
behind the thick swirl of his black hair,
the mole of wisdom,
a lone planet spinning slowly.

Sometimes my love is melancholy
and I hold her head in my hands.
Sometimes I recall our hair grows after death.
Then, I must grab handfuls
of her hair, and, I tell you, there
are apples, walnuts, ships sailing, ships docking, and men
taking off their boots, their hearts breaking,
not knowing
which they love more, the water, or
their women's hair, sprouting from the head, rushing toward
      the feet.

Early in the Morning

While the long grain is softening
in the water, gurgling
over a low stove flame, before
the salted Winter Vegetable is sliced
for breakfast, before the birds,
my mother glides an ivory comb
through her hair, heavy
and black as calligrapher's ink.

She sits at the foot of the bed.
My father watches, listens for
the music of comb
against hair.

My mother combs,
pulls her hair back
tight, rolls it
around two fingers, pins it
in a bun to the back of her head.
For half a hundred years she has done this.
My father likes to see it like this.
He says it is kempt.

But I know
it is because of the way
my mother's hair falls
when he pulls the pins out.
Easily, like the curtains
when they untie them in the evening.

Irises

1

In the night, in the wind, at the edge of the rain,
I find five irises, and call them lovely.
As if a woman, once, lay by them awhile,
then woke, rose, went, the memory of hair
lingers on their sweet tongues.

I'd like to tear these petals with my teeth.
I'd like to investigate these hairy selves,
their beauty and indifference. They hold
their breath all their lives
and open, open.

2

We are not lovers, not brother and sister,
though we drift hand in hand through a hall
thrilling and burning as thought and desire
expire, and, over this dream of life,
this life of sleep, we waken dying –
violet becoming blue, growing
black, black – all that
an iris ever prays,
when it prays,
to be.

Eating Alone

I've pulled the last of the year's young onions.
The garden is bare now. The ground is cold,
brown and old. What is left of the day flames
in the maples at the corner of my
eye. I turn, a cardinal vanishes.
By the cellar door, I wash the onions,
then drink from the icy metal spigot.

Once, years back, I walked beside my father
among the windfall pears. I can't recall
our words. We may have strolled in silence. But
I still see him bend that way – left hand braced
on knee, creaky – to lift and hold to my
eye a rotten pear. In it, a hornet
spun crazily, glazed in slow, glistening juice.

It was my father I saw this morning
waving to me from the trees. I almost
called to him, until I came close enough
to see the shovel, leaning where I had
left it, in the flickering, deep green shade.

White rice steaming, almost done. Sweet green peas
fried in onions. Shrimp braised in sesame
oil and garlic. And my own loneliness.
What more could I, a young man, want.

Always a Rose

1

What shape floats
in the dark window, what
ragged form?
Mouth, scream, edges
barbed, it balances
on a long, spiked, crooked
stem. I know now,
as if I'd never known, this
black shape within the night's black shape.

Dead daisies, shrivelled lilies, withered bodies
of dry chrysanthemums. Among these, and waste leaves
of yellow and brown fronds of palm and fern,
I came, and found
a rose
left for dead, heaped with the hopeless dead,
its petals still supple.
Of my brothers
one would have ignored it,
another ravished it, the third
would have pinned it to his chest and swaggered home.
My sister would rival its beauty,
my mother bow before it, then bear it
to my father's grave, where
he would grant it seven days,
then return and claim it forever.
I took it,
put it in water,
and set it on my windowsill.

2

In the procession of summers and the arrivals of days
the roses marched by in a blur: the roses burning
in the coffin between my father's stiff hands.

The rose I mistook for blood on my sister's breast.
A red rose I thought was a mouth (it was mute),
a white rose I swore was my soul (it choked).
Black Chinese roses my grandmother
describes to anyone who'll listen;
the ones that tasted like grapes
when she ate them as a girl.
Terrible rose my brother inherited,
worm-eaten rose
of his brain, rose
of ruin in his poor life.
And it was roses that broke the back of the Book of Martyrs,
and roses my mother would touch and heal, but roses
which went on dying.

Always a rose,
in prayer and in fever,
in the sun and in the den.
Always that doomed, profane flower, that vertical flame
darkens my arrivals, announces my departures,
and sweetens my dying.
Always the blackening, the bruising, the late fragrance,
the opening to fullness and toward death.
Always a rose ready
to spill its petals, so that I must pluck
each of them, or crush
the whole thing in my fist.
Or I must cup it
in my hands, adore it, in silence,
or, more often,
in words.

   3

When with arrows, night pierces you, rose,
I see most clearly
your true nature.
Small, auroral, your death is large.
You live, you die with me, in spite
of me, like my sleeping wife.

Lying here, with her at my right and you at my left,
the dying lies between the dying.

Bend closer, let me translate my nights and days.
Each finger is a brother or sister,
in each thumb is smudged the deaths I'm losing count of.
The left palm is the forsythia that never waved goodbye,
the right is my beloved pine dying from something no one knew.
My arms and legs are the rain in its opulence,
my face my mother's face.
My hair is also hers.
She inherited it from the horses
who recovered it from the night.
Here is what is left: a little brown, bits of black, a few specks
       of light.
Here are my shoulders and their winglessness,
my spine, the arc of love.
And here on my belly
is a stripe of skin, hairless
and the color of old blood.
Beginning at the navel, it descends into the tangled hairs.
Vestige, omen, this is the stain
which at my birth my father
traced with his finger
while pronouncing in dread
that I was born half girl.
So I was given the remedy of the rose,
made to eat you whole, swallow your medicinal taste.

Before the honey, before
the salty crystal,
I knew your bitterness,
a fresh shovel of dirt,
a bitterness rich with grief,
a black flavor far back in the throat,
one part soil, two parts root, and all the filaments of rain.
Question and answer in one
bud unfolding, you are what
the spade tastes with its sharp tongue,

what the earth utters in serious savors
more generous than salt, more memorable than sweetness,
something with a shadow the weight of a man
fallen asleep during incessant prayer,
a good, grave, exquisite
bitterness.

4

Odorous and tender flower-
body, I eat you
to recall my first misfortune.
Little, bitter
body, I eat you
to understand my grave father.
Excellent body of layers tightly
wound around nothing,
I eat you to put my faith in grief.
Singed at the edges, dying
from the flame you live by, I
eat you to sink into
my own body. Secret body
of deep liquor,
I eat you
down to your secret.

5

Listen now to something human.
I know moments measured
by a kiss, or a tear, a pass of the hand along a loved one's face.
I know lips that love me,
that return my kisses
by leaving on my cheek their salt.
And there is one I love, who hid her heart behind a stone.
Let there be a rose for her, who was poor,
who lived through ten bad years, and then ten more,
who took a lifetime to drain her bitter cup.
And there is one I love, smallest among us –
let there be a rose for him –
who was driven from the foreign schoolyards

by fists and yelling, who trembled in anger in each re-telling,
who played alone all the days,
though the afternoon trees were full of children.
And there is one I love who limps over this planet,
dragging her steel hip.
Always a rose for her.
And always a rose for one I love, lost
in another country, from whom I get year-old letters.
And always a rose for one I love
exiled from one republic and daily defeated in another,
who was shunned by brothers and stunned by God,
who couldn't sleep because of voices,
who raised his voice, then his hand
against his children, against his children
going. For him a rose, my lover of roses and of God,
who taught me to love the rose, and fed me roses, under whose
    windows
I planted roses, for whose tables I harvested roses,
who put his hand on my crown and purified me
in the name of the Father, of the Son, and of the Holy Ghost,
who said, *Get out! You're no longer my son!*
who never said, *Forgive me. Why do I die? Hold me, hold me.*
My father the Godly, he was the chosen.
My father almighty, full of good fear.
My father exhausted, my beloved.
My father among the roses and thorns.
My father rose, my father thorn.

6

Not for the golden pears, rotten on the ground –
their sweetness their secret – not for the scent
of their dying did I go back to my father's house. Not for the grass
grown wild as his beard in his last months,
nor for the hard, little apples that littered the yard,
and vines, rampant on the porch, tying the door shut,
did I stand there, late, rain arriving.
The rain came. And where there is rain
there is time, and memory, and sometimes sweetness.
Where there is a son there is a father.

And if there is love there is
no forgetting, but regret rending
two shaggy hearts.
I said goodbye to the forsythia, flowerless for years.
I turned from the hive-laden pine.
Then, I saw it – you, actually.
Past the choked rhododendrons,
behind the perishing gladiolas, there
in the far corner of the yard, you, my rose,
lovely for nothing, lonely for no one,
stunning the afternoon
with your single flower ablaze.
I left that place, I let the rain
meditate on the brilliance of one blossom
quivering in the beginning downpour.

7

Why do you stay away from me?
At what far edge
do you linger, trembler,
that you can't hear me call?
What is this liturgy, this
invocation, and to whom?
What are you to me? I'd tear you with my teeth!
Speak, speaking-flower!
Open me, thorn-flower!
Let me hear the grumbling of my fathers and uncles, blood
drop of my dead brother!

Still you say nothing.
So keep secret, secret. But
return to me, ever-returning.
And come inside, visitor, old rose, older than the remedy of the rose,
keeper of the back door, born
of sleep and the igneous kiss,
fed by what dies, rots, putrefies –
blood, pork-fat, and bone, fish-head,
shavings, peelings, curdled milk, what molds,
and stinks, this and the last and the last

year's leaves, mown grass, rotten apples, dead roses —
what I will not eat, but heap
on you in fall, each fall, that you may flourish,
ashen herald, that I may eat you, old
bitter rose.

8

If with my mouth,
if with my clumsy tongue, my teeth,
if with my voice, my voice
of little girl, of man, of blood, and if
with blood, if with marrow, if with groin, lungs,
if with breath bristling with animal and vegetable, if with all
the beast in me, all the beauty,
I form one word,
then another, one
word
for every moment
which passes, and if I do so until
all words are spoken, then
begin again,
if I adore you, Rose,
with adoration become nonsense become
praise, could I stop our dying?
Could we sit together in new bodies, shoulder to tender shoulder,
the lovely and the thorned, the bitter and the failed,
the grave to the left of us, the sea to the right?
Could you rise and stand and bear
the weight of all the names I would give you?
Cup of Blood, Old Wrath, Heart O' Mine, Ancient of Days,
Whorl, World, Word.
O day, come!

9

You sag,
turn your face
from me, body
made of other bodies, each doomed.

Remember it was I who bled for you, I, born
hungry among the hungry,
third in the last generation of the old country,
of the family Plum, a brood
distinguished by madness,
tales of chains and wailing.

It was I who saw you withered and discarded,
I, who taught my father patience, and dulled the blade of his anger,
who eat you now, before morning,
when you must climb your ladder of thorns and grow to death.
I, middle stone in the row of stones
on my mother's ring, I,
the flawed stone, saw you dying
and revived you. I saw you
dying and called you mine.
I named you each day you remained:
Scorn, Banish, Grieve, Forgive, Love.

10

My meditation, my recitative,
I love you best this way,
an old brittle trumpet,
a shred of my mother's dress, no longer regal.
I love your nakedness.
Naked, shy flower, sweet
to my nose, and bitter
to my tongue, among
the dying things
are you and I.

Eating Together

In the steamer is the trout
seasoned with slivers of ginger,
two sprigs of green onion, and sesame oil.
We shall eat it with rice for lunch,
brothers, sister, my mother who will
taste the sweetest meat of the head,
holding it between her fingers
deftly, the way my father did
weeks ago. Then he lay down
to sleep like a snow-covered road
winding through pines older than him,
without any travelers, and lonely for no one.

I Ask My Mother to Sing

She begins, and my grandmother joins her.
Mother and daughter sing like young girls.
If my father were alive, he would play
his accordion and sway like a boat.

I've never been in Peking, or the Summer Palace,
nor stood on the great Stone Boat to watch
the rain begin on Kuen Ming Lake, the picnickers
running away in the grass.

But I love to hear it sung;
how the waterlilies fill with rain until
they overturn, spilling water into water,
then rock back, and fill with more.

Both women have begun to cry.
But neither stops her song.

Mnemonic

I was tired. So I lay down.
My lids grew heavy. So I slept.
Slender memory, stay with me.

I was cold once. So my father took off his blue sweater.
He wrapped me in it, and I never gave it back.
It is the sweater he wore to America,
this one, which I've grown into, whose sleeves are too long,
whose elbows have thinned, who outlives its rightful owner.
Flamboyant blue in daylight, poor blue by daylight,
it is black in the folds.

A serious man who devised complex systems of numbers and
    rhymes
to aid him in remembering, a man who forgot nothing, my father
would be ashamed of me.
Not because I'm forgetful,
but because there is no order
to my memory, a heap
of details, uncatalogued, illogical.
For instance:
God was lonely. So he made me.
My father loved me. So he spanked me.
It hurt him to do so. He did it daily.

The earth is flat. Those who fall off don't return.
The earth is round. All things reveal themselves to men only
    gradually.

I won't last. Memory is sweet.
Even when it's painful, memory is sweet.

Once, I was cold. So my father took off his blue sweater.

Between Seasons

Today I bring you cold chrysanthemums,
white as absence, long-stemmed as my grief.
I stand before your grave, a few unfallen
leaves overhead, the sucking mud beneath.

What survives best are chrysanthemums
in a month which arrives austere as grief.
The hearty blossoms persevere, unfallen.
Suffering even snow, they flourish beneath.

You walked in mornings among chrysanthemums,
and bowed to them as if to hear their grief.
Your sleeves grew damp from brushing unfallen
dew. A drop lay by your eye, and one beneath.

Truest to your nature were chrysanthemums,
brilliant while first snows descended like grief.
You watched them from your bed, your heart unfallen,
steadfast through winter, and then you slipped beneath.

What is it they told you, once, the chrysanthemums?
It made you sigh, *Ah, Grief!*
Who savors you more than us, the unfallen,
long after we've forgotten the fallen beneath?

Visions and Interpretations

Because this graveyard is a hill,
I must climb up to see my dead,
stopping once midway to rest
beside this tree.

It was here, between the anticipation
of exhaustion, and exhaustion,
between vale and peak,
my father came down to me

and we climbed arm in arm to the top.
He cradled the bouquet I'd brought,
and I, a good son, never mentioned his grave,
erect like a door behind him.

And it was here, one summer day, I sat down
to read an old book. When I looked up
from the noon-lit page, I saw a vision
of a world about to come, and a world about to go.

Truth is, I've not seen my father
since he died, and, no, the dead
do not walk arm in arm with me.

If I carry flowers to them, I do so without their help,
the blossoms not always bright, torch-like,
but often heavy as sodden newspaper.

Truth is, I came here with my son one day,
and we rested against this tree,
and I fell asleep, and dreamed

a dream which, upon my boy waking me, I told.
Neither of us understood.
Then we went up.

Even this is not accurate.
Let me begin again:

Between two griefs, a tree.
Between my hands, white chrysanthemums, yellow chrysanthemums.

The old book I finished reading
I've since read again and again.

And what was far grows near,
and what is near grows more dear,

and all of my visions and interpretations
depend on what I see,

and between my eyes is always
the rain, the migrant rain.

from
THE CITY IN WHICH I LOVE YOU
(1990)

Furious Versions

1

These days I waken in the used light
of someone's spent life, to discover
the birds have stripped my various names of meaning entire:
the sparrow by quarrel,
the dove by grievance.
I lie
dismantled. I feel
the hours. Do they veer
to dusk? Or dawn?
Will I rise and go
out into an American city?
Or walk down to the wilderness sea?
I might run with wife and children to the docks
to bribe an officer for our lives
and perilous passage.
Then I'd answer
in an oceanic tongue
to *Professor, Capitalist, Husband, Father.*
Or I might have one more
hour of sleep before my father
comes to take me
to his snowbound church
where I dust the pews and he sets candles
out the color of teeth.
That means I was born in Bandung, 1958;
on my father's back, in borrowed clothes,
I came to America.

And I wonder
if I imagined those wintry mornings
in a dim nave, since
I'm the only one
who's lived to tell it,
and I confuse

the details; was it my father's skin
which shone like teeth?
Was it his heart that lay snowbound?
But if I waken to a jailer
rousting me to meet my wife and son,
come to see me in my cell
where I eat the chocolate
and smoke the cigarettes they smuggle,
what name do I answer to?
And did I stand
on the train from Chicago to Pittsburgh
so my fevered son could sleep? Or did I
open my eyes
and see my father's closed face
rocking above me?

Memory revises me.
Even now a letter
comes from a place
I don't know, from someone
with my name
and postmarked years ago,
while I await
injunctions from the light
or the dark;
I wait for shapeliness
limned, or dissolution.
Is paradise due or narrowly missed
until another thousand years?

I wait
in a blue hour
and faraway noise of hammering,
and on a page a poem begun, something
about to be dispersed,
something about to come into being.

2

I wake to black
and one sound –
neither a heart
approaching nor one shoe
coming, but something
less measured, never
arriving. I wander
a house I thought I knew;
I walk the halls as if the halls
of that other
mansion, my father's heart.
I follow the sound
past a black window
where a bird sits like a blacker
question, *To where? To where? To where?*
Past my mother's room where her
knees creak, *Meaning. Meaning.*
While a rose
rattles at my ear, *Where
is your father?*
And the silent house
booms, *Gone. Long gone.*

A door jumps
out from shadows,
then jumps away. This
is what I've come to find:
the back door, unlatched.
Tooled by an insular wind, it
slams and slams
without meaning
to and without meaning.

3

Moonlight and high wind.
Dark poplars toss, insinuate the sea.
The yard heaves, perplexed
with shadows massed
and with shadows falling away.
Before me a tree, distinct
in its terrible
aspects, emerges, reels, sinks,
and is lost.
At my feet, shapes
tear free, separate darknesses
mingle, then crawl to the common
dark, lost.
At the brink
of my own now-here, now-gone
shadow stand three flowers,
or two flowers,
and one's shade.
Impatiens? Alyssum?
Something forbids me to speak
of them in this
upheaval of forms and
voices – there are voices
now, plaintive, anxious.
I hear
interrogation in vague tongues.
I hear ocean sounds and a history of rain.
Somewhere a streetlamp,
and my brother never coming.
Somewhere a handful of hair and a lost box of letters.
And everywhere, fire,
corridors of fire, brick and barbed wire.

Soldiers sweep the streets
for my father. My mother
hides him, haggard,
in the closet.

The booted ones herd us
to the sea.
Waves furl, boats
and bodies drift out, farther out.
My father holds my hand, he says,
Don't forget any of this.
A short, bony-faced corporal
asks politely, deferring to class,
*What color suit, Professor, would you like
to be buried in? Brown or blue?*
A pistol butt turns my father's spit to blood.

It was a tropical night.
It was a half a year of sweat and fatal memory.
It was one year of fire
out of the world's diary of fires,
flesh-laced, mid-century fire,
teeth and hair infested,
napalm-dressed and skull-hung fire,
and imminent fire, an elected
fire come to rob me
of my own death, my damp bed
in the noisy earth,
my rocking toward a hymn-like night.

How, then, may I
speak of flowers
here, where
a world of forms convulses,

here, amidst
drafts — yet
these are not drafts
toward a future form, but
furious versions
of the here and now...

Here, now, one
should say nothing
of three flowers,
only enter with them
in silence, fear, and hope,
into the next nervous one hundred human years.

4

But I see these flowers, and they seize
my mind, and I
can no more un-see
them than I can un-dream
this, no more than
the mind can stop
its wandering over the things
of the world, snagged on the world
as it is.
The mind is
a flowering
cut into time,
a rose,

the wandering rose
that scaled the red brick
of my father's house in Pennsylvania.
What was its name?
Each bloom, unsheathed
in my mind, urges, *Remember!*
The Paul's Scarlet!
Paul, who promised the coming
of the perfect and the departing of the imperfect,
Else why stand we in jeopardy every hour?

I thought of Paul
the morning I stepped out my door
and into an explosion of wings,
thudding and flapping, heavenly blows.

Blinded, I knew the day
of fierce judgement and rapture
had come. I thought
even the dooryard rose,
touched by wind, trembling
in anticipation
of first petal-fall,

announcement of death's commencement,
would take back
its flowering, claim glory.
So the rose and I
stood, terrified, at the beginning
of a new and beloved era.

It was pigeons, only pigeons
I'd startled from the porch rafters.
But the dread and hope
I carry with me
like lead and wings
let me believe otherwise.

True, none of this
has to do with heaven, since the sight
of those heavy birds flying away
reminded me
not so much of what's to come
as of what passes
away: birds,
hours, words, gestures, persons,
a drowned guitar in spring,
smell of lacquered wood
and wax when I prayed as a boy,
a pale check cut
by a green leaf,

the taste of blood
in a kiss,
someone whispering into someone's ear,
someone crying behind a door,
a clock dead at noon.
My father's hand
cupping my chin, weighing
tenderness between us,
pressing my mother's hip, weighing desire,
and cleaving a book open.
On the right of his hand, the words:

The Song of Songs, which is Solomon's.
Let him kiss me with the kisses of his mouth.
On the left of his hand the words:
For God shall bring every work
into judgement with every secret thing,
whether it be good,
or whether it be evil.
Outside his window, his rose,
aphid-eaten, bad-weather-wracked,
stem and thorn,
crook and bramble groping,
gripping brick, each sickly
bloom uttering, *I shall not die!*
before it's dispersed.

5

My father wandered,
me beside him, human,
erect, unlike
roses. And, unlike
Paul, we had no mission,
though he loved Paul, read him continually
as, republic to republic,
oligarchy to anarchy to democracy, we arrived.

Once, while I walked
with my father, a man
reached out, touched his arm, said, *Kuo Yuan?*
The way he stared and spoke my father's name,
I thought he meant to ask, *Are you a dream?*
Here was the sadness of ten thousand miles,
of an abandoned house in Nan Jing,
where my father helped a blind man
wash his wife's newly dead body,
then bury it, while bombs
fell, and trees raised
charred arms and burned.
Here was a man who remembered
the sound of another's footfalls
so well as to call to him
after twenty years
on a sidewalk in America.

America, where, in Chicago, Little Chinatown,
who should I see
on the corner of Argyle and Broadway
but Li Bai and Du Fu, those two
poets of the wanderer's heart.

Folding paper boats,
they sent them swirling
down little rivers of gutter water.
Gold-toothed, cigarettes rolled in their sleeves,
they noted my dumb surprise:
What did you expect? Where else should we be?

6

It goes on and it goes on,
the ceaseless invention, incessant
constructions and deconstructions
of shadows over black grass,
while, overhead, poplars
rock and nod,
wrestle *No* and *Yes*, contend
moon, no moon.
To think of the sea
is to hear in the sound of trees
the sound of the sea's work,
the wave's labor to change
the shore, not for the shore's sake, nor the wave's,
certainly not for me,
hundreds of miles from sea,
unless you count
my memory, my traverse
of sea one way to here.
I'm like my landlocked poplars: far
from water, I'm full of the sound of water.

But sea-sound differs from the sound of trees:
it owns a rhythm, almost
a meaning, but
no human story,
and so is like
the sound of trees,
tirelessly building
as wind builds, rising
as wind rises, steadily gathering
to nothing, quiet, and
the wind rising again.

The night grows
miscellaneous in the sound of trees.

But I own a human story,
whose very telling
remarks loss.

The characters survive through the telling,
the teller survives
by his telling; by his voice
brinking silence does he survive.
But, no one
can tell without cease
our human
story, and so we
lose, lose.

Yet, behind the sound
of trees is another
sound. Sometimes, lying
awake, or standing
like this in the yard, I hear it. It
ties our human telling
to its course
by momentum, and ours
is merely part
of its unbroken
stream, the human
and otherwise simultaneously
told. The past
doesn't fall away, the past
joins the greater
telling, and is.

At times its theme seems
murky, other times clear. Always,
death is a phrase, but just
a phrase, since nothing is ever
lost, and lives
are fulfilled by subsequence.
Listen, you can hear it: indescribable,
neither grief nor joy, neither mine nor yours…

But I'll not widow the world.
I'll tell my human
tale, tell it against
the current of that vaster, that
inhuman telling.
I'll measure time by losses and destructions.
Because the world
is so rich in detail, all of it so frail;
because all I love is imperfect;
because my memory's flaw
isn't in retention but organisation;
because no one asked.

I'll tell once and for all
how someone lived.
Born on an island ruled by a petty soldier,
he was wrapped in bright cloth
and bound to his mother's hip,
where he rode until he could walk.
He did not utter a sound his first three years,
and his parents frowned.
Then, on the first night of their first exile,
he spoke out in complete sentences,
a Malaysian so lovely it was true song.

But when he spoke again
it was plain, artless, and twenty years later.
He wore a stranger's clothes,
he married a woman who tasted of iron and milk.
They had two sons, the namesakes
of a great emperor and a good-hearted bandit.
And always he stood erect to praise or grieve,
and knelt to live a while
at the level of his son's eyes.

7

Tonight, someone, unable
to see in one darkness,
has shut his eyes
to see into another.
Among the sleepers, he is one
who doesn't sleep
Know him by his noise.
Hear the nervous
scratching of his pencil,
sound of a rasping
file, a small
restless percussion, a soul's
minute chewing,
the old poem
birthing itself
into the new
and murderous century.

The Interrogation

Two streams: one dry, one poured all night by our beds.

I'll wonder
about neither.

The dry one was clogged with bodies.

I'm through
with memory.

At which window of what house did light teach you tedium?
On which step of whose stairway did you learn indecision?

I'm through
sorting avenues and doors,
curating houses and deaths.

Which house did we flee by night? Which house did we flee by day?

Don't ask me.

We stood and watched one burn; from one we ran away.

I'm neatly folding
the nights and days, notes
to be forgotten.

We were diminished. We were not spared. There was no pity.
Neither was their sanctuary. Neither rest.
There were fires in the streets. We stood among men, at the level
of their hands, all those wrists, dead or soon to die.

No more
letting my survival
depend on memory.

There was the sea; its green volume brought despair.
There was waiting, there was leaving. There was
astonishment too. The astonishment of
'I thought you died!' 'How did you get out?'
'And Little Fei Fei walked right by the guards!'

I grow
leaden with stories,
my son's eyelids
grow heavy.

Who rowed the boat when our father tired?

Don't ask me.

Who came along? Who got left behind?

Ask the sea.

Through it all there was no song, and weeping
came many years later.

I'm through
with memory.

Sometimes a song,
even when there was weeping.

I'm through with memory.

Can't you still smell the smoke on my body?

This Hour and What Is Dead

Tonight my brother, in heavy boots, is walking
through bare rooms over my head,
opening and closing doors.
What could he be looking for in an empty house?
What could he possibly need there in heaven?
Does he remember his earth, his birthplace set to torches?
His love for me feels like spilled water
running back to its vessel.

At this hour, what is dead is restless
and what is living is burning.

Someone tell him he should sleep now.

My father keeps a light on by our bed
and readies for our journey.
He mends ten holes in the knees
of five pairs of boy's pants.
His love for me is like his sewing:
various colors and too much thread,
the stitching uneven. But the needle pierces
clean through with each stroke of his hand.

At this hour, what is dead is worried
and what is living is fugitive.

Someone tell him he should sleep now.

God, that old furnace, keeps talking
with his mouth of teeth,
a beard stained at feasts, and his breath
of gasoline, airplane, human ash.
His love for me feels like fire,
feels like doves, feels like river-water.

At this hour, what is dead is helpless, kind
and helpless. While the Lord lives.

Someone tell the Lord to leave me alone.
I've had enough of his love
that feels like burning and flight and running away.

This Room and Everything in It

Lie still now
while I prepare for my future,
certain hard days ahead,
when I'll need what I know so clearly this moment.

I am making use
of the one thing I learned
of all the things my father tried to teach me:
the art of memory.

I am letting this room
and everything in it
stand for my ideas about love
and its difficulties.

I'll let your love-cries,
those spacious notes
of a moment ago,
stand for distance.

Your scent,
that scent
of spice and a wound,
I'll let stand for mystery.

Your sunken belly
is the daily cup
of milk I drank
as a boy before morning prayer.

The sun on the face
of the wall
is God, the face
I can't see, my soul,

and so on, each thing
standing for a separate idea,
and those ideas forming the constellation
of my greater idea.
And one day, when I need
to tell myself something intelligent
about love,

I'll close my eyes
and recall this room and everything in it:
My body is estrangement.
This desire, perfection.
Your closed eyes my extinction.
Now I've forgotten my
idea. The book
on the windowsill, riffled by wind...
the even-numbered pages are
the past, the odd-
numbered pages, the future.
The sun is
God, your body is milk...

useless, useless...
your cries are song, my body's not me...
no good...my idea
has evaporated...your hair is time, your thighs are song...
it had something to do
with death...it had something
to do with love.

The City in Which I Love You

> *I will arise now, and go*
> *about the city in the streets,*
> *and in the broad ways I will seek...*
> *whom my soul loveth.*
>   SONGS OF SONGS 3:2

And when, in the city in which I love you,
even my most excellent song goes unanswered,
and I mount the scabbed streets,
the long shouts of avenues,
and tunnel sunken night in search of you...

That I negotiate fog, bituminous
rain ringing like teeth into the beggar's tin,
or two men jackaling a third in some alley
weirdly lit by a couch on fire, that I
drag my extinction in search of you...

Past the guarded schoolyards, the boarded-up churches, swastikaed
synagogues, defended houses of worship, past
newspapered windows of tenements, among the violated,
the prosecuted citizenry, throughout this
storied, buttressed, scavenged, policed
city I call home, in which I am a guest...

A bruise, blue
in the muscle, you
impinge upon me.
As bone hugs the ache home, so
I'm vexed to love you, your body

the shape of returns, your hair a torso
of light, your heat
I must have, your opening
I'd eat, each moment
of that soft-finned fruit,
inverted fountain in which I don't see me.

My tongue remembers your wounded flavor.
The vein in my neck
adores you. A sword
stands up between my hips,
my hidden fleece sends forth its scent of human oil.

The shadows under my arms,
I promise, are tender, the shadows
under my face. Do not calculate,
but come, smooth other, rough sister.
Yet, how will you know me

among the captives, my hair grown long,
my blood motley, my ways trespassed upon?
In the uproar, the confusion
of accents and inflections,
how will you hear me when I open my mouth?

Look for me, one of the drab population
under fissured edifices, fractured
artifices. Make my various
names flock overhead,
I will follow you.
Hew me to your beauty.

Stack in me the unaccountable fire,
bring on me the iron leaf, but tenderly.
Folded one hundred times and
creased, I'll not crack.
Threshed to excellence, I'll achieve you.

But in the city
in which I love you,
no one comes, no one
meets me in the brick clefts;
in the wedged dark,

no finger touches me secretly, no mouth
tastes my flawless salt,
no one wakens the honey in the cells, finds the humming
in the ribs, the rich business in the recesses;
hulls clogged, I continue laden, translated

by exhaustion and time's appetite, my sleep abandoned
in bus stations and storefront stoops,
my insomnia erected under a sky
cross-hatched by wires, branches,
and black flights of rain. Lewd body of wind

jams me in the passageways, doors slam
like guns going off, a gun goes off, a pie plate spins
past, whizzing its thin tremolo,
a plastic bag, fat with wind, barrels by and slaps
a chain-link fence, wraps it like clung skin.

In the excavated places,
I waited for you, and I did not cry out.
In the derelict rooms, my body needed you,
and there was such flight in my breast.
During the daily assaults, I called to you,

and my voice pursued you,
even backward
to that other city
in which I saw a woman
squat in the street

beside a body,
and fan with a handkerchief flies from its face.
That woman
was not me. And
the corpse

lying there, lying there
so still it seemed with great effort, as though
his whole being was concentrating on the hole
in his forehead, so still
I expected he'd sit up any minute and laugh out loud:

that man was not me;
his wound was his, his death not mine.
And the soldier
who fired the shot, then lit a cigarette:
he was not me.

And the ones I do not see
in cities all over the world,
the ones sitting, standing, lying down, those
in prisons playing checkers with their knocked-out teeth:
they are not me. Some of them are

my age, even my height and weight;
none of them is me.
The woman who is slapped, the man who is kicked,
the ones who don't survive,
whose names I do not know;

they are not me forever,
the ones who no longer live
in the cities in which
you are not,
the cities in which I looked for you.

The rain stops, the moon
in her breaths appears overhead.
The only sound now is a far flapping.
Over the National Bank, the flag of some republic or other
gallops like water or fire to tear itself away.

If I feel the night
move to disclosures or crescendos,
it's only because I'm famished
for meaning; the night
merely dissolves.

And your otherness is perfect as my death.
Your otherness exhausts me,
like looking suddenly up from here
to impossible stars fading.
Everything is punished by your absence.

Is prayer, then, the proper attitude
for the mind that longs to be freely blown,
but which gets snagged on the barb
called *world*, that
toothache, the actual? What prayer

would I build? And to whom?
Where are you
in the cities in which I love you,
the cities daily risen to work and to money,
to the magnificent miles and the gold coasts?

Morning comes to this city, vacant of you.
Pages and windows flare, and you are not there.
Someone sweeps his portion of sidewalk,
wakens the drunk, slumped like laundry,
and you are gone.

You are not in the wind
which someone notes in the margins of a book.
You are gone out of the small fires in abandoned lots
where human figures huddle,
each aspiring to its own ghost.

Between brick walls, in a space no wider than my face,
a leafless sapling stands in mud.
In its branches, a nest of raw mouths
gaping and cheeping, scrawny fires that must eat.
My hunger for you is no less than theirs.

At the gates of the city in which I love you,
the sea hauls the sun on its back,
strikes the land, which rebukes it.
What ardor in its sliding heft,
a flameless friction on the rocks.

Like the sea, I am recommended by my orphaning.
Noisy with telegrams not received,
quarrelsome with aliases,
intricate with misguided journeys,
by my expulsions have I come to love you.

Straight from my father's wrath,
and long from my mother's womb,
late in this century and on a Wednesday morning,
bearing the mark of one who's experienced
neither heaven nor hell,

my birthplace vanished, my citizenship earned,
in league with stones of the earth, I
enter, without retreat or help from history,
the days of no day, my earth
of no earth, I re-enter

the city in which I love you.
And I never believed that the multitude
of dreams and many words were vain.

A Story

Sad is the man who is asked for a story
and can't come up with one.

His five-year-old son waits in his lap.
Not the same story, Baba. A new one.
The man rubs his chin, scratches his ear.

In a room full of books in a world
of stories, he can recall
not one, and soon, he thinks, the boy
will give up on his father.

Already the man lives far ahead, he sees
the day this boy will go. *Don't go!*
Hear the alligator story! The angel story once more!
You love the spider story. You laugh at the spider.
Let me tell it!

But the boy is packing his shirts,
he is looking for his keys. *Are you a god,*
the man screams, *that I sit mute before you?*
Am I a god that I should never disappoint?

But the boy is here. *Please, Baba, a story?*
It is an emotional rather than logical equation,
an earthly rather than heavenly one,
which posits that a boy's supplications
and a father's love add up to silence.

Goodnight

You've stopped whispering
and are asleep. I go on listening

to apples drop in the grass
beyond the window. Earlier we tried to guess

each fall's moment, but neither kept up
that little game of hope

or fear for long. Now, your weight
against me is like...I was about to say

like no other, unmistakably
human, my son's. But, truth is, you're simply

heft. Burden like, say, grain,
your body brings my body pain,

your shoulders, knees, elbows, hands,
lumpy like sacked fruit, and

whatever concord is
actual between us is

not easily meant,
but is so only by our diligence.

I recall a far
season of flowers

when, for love, I crept to the edge of a roof to reach
a petal-decked branch.

It snapped, I
dropped, screaming down sky

and flowering. My father yelled
my name, ran out to find me sprawled,

dazed, gripping his crushed gift, thrust
at him in my bloody fist.

He plunges below us now, as we
fall soundless toward him, our bodies

crowded on your narrow bed,
my arm and leg gone numb, your torso wedged

between the wall and me.
You sleep uncomfortably,

though comforted by my
presence, for which you cry

some nights, and which you, such nights, endure.
Where did you, so young, learn

such sacrifice? Now
I no longer hear the apples fall. But how

they go! Incessantly, though
with no noise, no

blunt announcements of their gravity.
See!

There is no bottom to the night, no end
to our descent.

We suffer each other to have each other a while.

You Must Sing

He sings in his father's arms, sings his father
to sleep, all the while seeing how on that face
grown suddenly strange, wasting to shadow,
time moves. Stern time. Sweet time. Because his father

asked, he sings; because they are wholly lost.
How else, in immaculate noon, will each find
each, who are so close now? So close and lost.
His voice stands at windows, runs everywhere.

Was death giant? O, how will he find his
father? They are so close. Was death a guest?
By which door did it come? All the day's doors
are closed. He must go out of those hours, that house,

the enfolding limbs, go burdened to learn:
you must sing to be found; when found, you must sing.

Here I Am

I wait. I don't go. He will come, the one
who waited for me each day
at the edge of the schoolyard.

I wait. And I am bitten thin
by waiting. And I grow
dense with luggage and time.

He will come, though
he may never come, who wrote his name
by drawing a spear borne in a heart.

In this life, this is how
one must wait, past despair,
the heart a fossil, the minutes molten, the feet turned to stone.

I know a boy who fell asleep
one second before his father returned, his name
a lozenge thinning on his father's tongue.

I've heard of prisoners who died
a minute before rescue.
Such waiting has nothing to do with hope;

it has less to do with patience;
it's simply the way a soul is bent.
Such waiting is impossible.

But I wait,
for it's the only
possibility left to me.

And though I stopped waiting years ago,
I continue to wait.
Even now

he comes, whom death has made giant.
And small as the rain
and as many.

Whose Sabbath shoes
I blackened each Saturday
and buffed to hard armor.

Who set me on a chair and two dictionaries
and made me read an old book
of ancient and terrifying stories

while sucking butterscotch drops
he unwrapped for me.
Sweet learning, he called it.

Even now,
no one comes,
though I sense his pure approach.

Maybe he is lost,
the lonely one
who is no longer lonely.

Maybe he waits for me.
Maybe he fears he is forgotten,
the way I am forgotten,

each of us the one
who, in that childhood game, shouts,
though no one hears, *Here I am!*

from
BOOK OF MY NIGHTS
(2001)

Pillow

There's nothing I can't find under there.
Voices in the trees, the missing pages
of the sea.

Everything but sleep.

And night is a river bridging
the speaking and the listening banks,

a fortress, undefended and inviolate.

There's nothing that won't fit under it:
fountains clogged with mud and leaves,
the houses of my childhood.

And night begins when my mother's fingers
let go of the thread
they've been tying and untying
to touch toward our fraying story's hem.

Night is the shadow of my father's hands
setting the clock for resurrection.

Or is it the clock unraveled, the numbers flown?

There's nothing that hasn't found home there:
discarded wings, lost shoes, a broken alphabet.

Everything but sleep. And night begins

with the first beheading
of the jasmine, its captive fragrance
rid at last of burial clothes.

A Table in the Wilderness

I draw a window
and a man sitting inside it.

I draw a bird in flight above the lintel.

That's my picture of *thinking*.

If I put a woman there instead
of the man, it's a picture of *speaking*.

If I draw a second bird
in the woman's lap, it's *ministering*.

A third flying below her feet.
Now it's *singing*.

Or erase the birds,
make ivy branching
around the woman's ankles, clinging
to her knees, and it becomes *remembering*.

You'll have to find your own
pictures, whoever you are,
whatever your need.

As for me, many small hands
issuing from a waterfall
means silence
mothered me.

The hours hung like fruit in night's tree
means when I close my eyes
and look inside me,

a thousand open eyes
span the moment of my waking.

Meanwhile, the clock
adding a grain to a grain
and not getting bigger,

subtracting a day from a day
and never having less, means the honey

lies awake all night
inside the honeycomb
wondering who its parents are.

And even my death isn't my death
unless it's the unfathomed brow
of a nameless face.

Even my name isn't my name
except the bees assemble

a table to grant a stranger
light and moment in a wilderness
of *Who? Where?*

Hurry toward Beginning

Is it because the hour is late
the dove sounds new,

no longer asking
a path to its father's house,
no longer begging shoes of its mother?

Or is it because I can't tell departure
from arrival, the host from the guest,

the one who waits expectant at the window
from the one who, even now, tramples the dew?

I can't tell what my father said about the sea
we crossed together
from the sea itself,

or the rose's noon from my mother
crying on the stairs, lost
between a country and a country.

Everywhere is home to the rain.
The hours themselves, where do they hide?
The fruit of listening, what's that?

Are days the offspring of distracted hands?
Does waiting that grows out of waiting
grow lighter? What does my death weigh?
What's earlier, thirst or shade?
Is all light late, the echo to some prior bell?

Is it because I'm tired that I don't know?
Or is it because I'm dying?
When will I be born? Am I the flower,
wide awake inside the falling fruit?

Or a man waiting for a woman
asleep behind a door?
What if a word unlocks
room after room the days
wait inside? Still,

night amasses a foreground
current to my window.
Listen. Whose footsteps are those
hurrying toward beginning?

Little Round

My fool asks: Do the years spell a path to later
be remembered? Who's there to read them back?

My death says: One bird knows the hour and suffers
to house its millstone-weight as song.

My night watchman lies down
in a room by the sea
and hears the water telling,
out of a thousand mouths,
the story behind his mother's sleeping face.

My eternity shrugs and yawns:
Let the stars knit and fold
inside their numbered rooms. When night asks
who I am I answer, *Your own*, and am not lonely.

My loneliness, my sleepless darling
reminds herself
the fruit that falls increases
at the speed of the body rising to meet it.

And my child? He sleeps and sleeps.

And my mother? She divides
the rice, today's portion from tomorrow's,
tomorrow's from ever after.

And my father. He faces me and rows
toward what he can't see.

And my God.
What have I done with my God?

Where Art Thou?

Moving into a bigger house,
our voices wander

in the day, among new rooms, calling, *Where are you?*

And what we can't forget about other houses
confuses us,

as we answer back and forth, *I'm here!*

And what we don't understand about here
and there, relativity and moving bodies,

what's inside, what's outside,
what's me, what's you, confounds us,

destined to keep calling,
Where's here?
Should I come to you?
Are we closer?

It's a little like
returning to the village
where you were born. The sad bewilderment
of finding yourself

caught between
what's there and what you remember.
The happy confusion, the fear,
of letting go of both.

No. It's more like a memory of heaven.
Voices approaching, voices going away,

and what we thought we knew
about life on earth clouding us.

And then that question
from which all the other questions begin.

My Father's House

Here, as in childhood, Brother, no one sees us.
And someone has died, and someone is not yet born.

Our father walks through his church at night
and sets all the clocks for spring. His sleeplessness

weighs heavy on my forehead, his death almost
nothing. In the letter he never wrote to us

he says, *No one can tell how long it takes a seed
to declare what death and lightning told it*

*while it slept. But stand at a window long enough,
late enough, and you may some night hear*

*a secret you'll tomorrow, parallel to the morning,
tell on a wide, white bed, to a woman*

*like a sown ledge of wheat. Or you may never
tell it, who lean across the night and miles of the sea,*

*to arrive at a seed, in whose lamplit house
resides a thorn, or a wee man carving*

*a name on a stone, the name of the one who has died,
the name of the one not born unknown.*

Someone has died. Someone is not yet born.
And during this black interval,

I sweep all three floors of our father's house,
and I don't count the broom strokes; I row

up and down for nothing but love: his for me, my own
for the threshold, and for the woman's voice

I hear while I sweep, as though she swept beside me,
a woman whose face, if she owns a face at all,

is its own changing. And if I know her name
I know to say it so softly she need not

stop her work to hear me. Though when she lies down
at night, in the room of our arrival,

she'll know I called her.
And when she answers it's morning,

which even now is overwhelming, the woman
combing her hair opposite to my departure.

And only now and then do I lean at a jamb
to see if I can see what I thought I heard.

I heard her ask, *My love, why can't you sleep?*
and answer, *Someone has died, and someone*

is not yet born. Meanwhile, I hear the voices
of women telling a story in the round,

and I sit down on the rough stoop, by the sea grass,
and go on folding the laundry I was folding,

the everyday clothes of our everyday life, the death
clothes wearing us clean to the bone.

And I know the tide is rising early,
and I can't hope to trap the story

told in the round. But the woman I know
says, *Sleep*, so I lie down on the clothes,

the folded and unfolded, the life and the death.
Ages go by. When I wake, the story has changed

the firmament into domain, domain
into a house, and the sun speaks the day,

unnaming, showing the telling, dissipating
the boundaries of the story to include

the one who has died and the one not yet born.
How still the morning grows about the voice

of one child reading to another.
How much a house is house at all due

to one room where an elder child reads
to his brother. And the younger knows by heart

the brother-voice. How dark the other rooms,
how slow morning comes

collected in a name
told at one sill

and listened for at the threshold of dew.
What book is this we read

together, Brother, and at which window
of our father's house? In which upper room?

We read it twice: once in two voices, to each other,
and once in unison, to children

and the sun, our star, that vast office
we sit inside while birds lend their church

sown in air, realised in a body uttering
windows, growing rafters, couching seeds.

The Moon from Any Window

The moon from any window is one part
whoever's looking.

The part I can't see
is everything my sister keeps to herself.

One part my dead brother's sleepless brow,

the other part the time I waste, the time
I won't have.

But which is the lion
killed for the sake of the honey inside him,

and which the wine, stranded
in a valley, unredeemed?

And don't forget the curtains. Don't forget the wind
in the trees, or my mother's voice saying things
that will take my whole life to come true.

One part earnest child grown tall
in his mother's doorway, and one a last look
over the shoulder before leaving.

And never forget it answers to no address,
but calls wave after wave
to a path of thirst. Never forget

the candle climbing down
without glancing back.

And what about the heart
counting alone, out loud, in that game
in which the many hide from the one?

Never forget the cry
completely hollowed of the dying one
who cried it.

Only in such pure outpouring
is there room for all this night.

Our River Now

Say night is a house you inherit,
and in the room in which you hear the sea
declare its countless and successive deaths,
tolling the dimensions
of your own dying,

you close your eyes and dream
the king's bees build the king's honey
in the furthest reaches of your childhood.
Wouldn't you set your clocks
by that harvest?

And didn't you, a sleepless child
saying to yourself the name
your parents gave you
over and over, hear

both the ringing sum of you
such sound accounted for
and all the rest, the dumb
throng of you that never answered to a word,

that stands even now
assembled where your calling brinks,
the unutterable
luring your voice
out of its place of rocks
and into a multitude of waters?
But what was it I meant to say? Something

about our beginningless past.
Maybe. Maybe our river,
folding story with forgetting,
dreams out loud.

The Bridge

The stars report a vast consequence
our human moment joins.

Or is it all the dark
around them speaking?

And if someone who listened for years
one night hears *Home*,

what is he to do with the story
his bones hum to him
about the dust?

Let him go in search of the hiding place
of the dew, where the hours are born.

Let him uncover whose heart
beats behind the falling leaves.

And as for the one who hears *Remember*,

well, I began to sing
the words my father sang
when he knelt to teach me
how to tie my shoes:

*Crossing over, crossing under, little bird,
build your bridge by nightfall.*

Words for Worry

Another word for father is *worry*.

Worry boils the water
for tea in the middle of the night.

Worry trimmed the child's nails before
singing him to sleep.

Another word for *son* is *delight*,
another word, *hidden*.

And another is *One-Who-Goes-Away*.
Yet another, *One-Who-Returns*.

So many words for son:
He-Dreams-for-All-Our-Sakes.
His-Play-Vouchsafes-Our-Winter-Share.
His-Dispersal-Wins-the-Birds.

But only one word for *father*.
And sometimes a man is both.
Which is to say sometimes a man
manifests mysteries beyond
his own understanding.

For instance, being the one and the many,
and the loneliness of either. Or

the living light we see by, we never see. Or

the sole word weighs
heavy as a various name.

And sleepless worry folds the laundry for tomorrow.
Tired worry wakes the child for school.

Orphan worry writes the note he hides
in the child's lunch bag.
It begins, *Dear Firefly*…

Little Father

I buried my father
in the sky.
Since then, the birds
clean and comb him every morning
and pull the blanket up to his chin
every night.

I buried my father underground.
Since then, my ladders
only climb down,
and all the earth has become a house
whose rooms are the hours, whose doors
stand open at evening, receiving
guest after guest.
Sometimes I see past them
to the tables spread for a wedding feast.

I buried my father in my heart.
Now he grows in me, my strange son,
my little root who won't drink milk,
little pale foot sunk in unheard-of night,
little clock spring newly wet
in the fire, little grape, parent to the future
wine, a son the fruit of his own son,
little father I ransom with my life.

Build by Flying

I lean on a song.
I follow a story.
I keep my mother waiting
when she asks, *How long
before the wren finishes the grain?
How soon until we see
what a house the birds
build by flying?* In the dream
in which I stopped with her
under branches, on the long way home from school,
one of us, curious
about the fruit overhead, asked:
*To what port has the fragrance so lately
embarked, for whose tables?*
One of us waited for the answer.
And one went on alone,
singing. And all the place
there was grew out of listening.

In the Beginning

A woman is speaking in a place of rocks.

Her voice is the water of that place
and founds the time there.

She says World and Mind
arise simultaneously. Mind, she says,
begun out of nothing,
stands by turning

out of grasp, a lover's *yes* and *no*,
stay and go, singing stepping
in and out of time and momentum.

World, she says, world
is the body's doctrine
of need and scarcity manifest,

the heart's full measure
of night and day, sons and daughters.

A woman is talking. Her voice
is a boat and oars in a place of rocks.

Stranded in a rocky place,
it is a garment torn to pieces.

It is the light,
accomplished by wind and fire,
abiding inside the rocks.

A memory of the sea, it's what remains.
Homesickness in the rocks.
Homecoming in the trees.

The Hammock

When I lay my head in my mother's lap
I think how day hides the stars,
the way I lay hidden once, waiting
inside my mother's singing to herself. And I remember
how she carried me on her back
between home and the kindergarten,
once each morning and once each afternoon.

I don't know what my mother's thinking.

When my son lays his head in my lap, I wonder:
Do his father's kisses keep his father's worries
from becoming his? I think, *Dear God*, and remember
there are stars we haven't heard from yet:
They have so far to arrive. *Amen*,
I think, and I feel almost comforted.

I've no idea what my child is thinking.

Between two unknowns, I live my life.
Between my mother's hopes, older than I am
by coming before me, and my child's wishes, older than I am
by outliving me. And what's it like?
Is it a door, and goodbye on either side?
A window, and eternity on either side?
Yes, and a little singing between two great rests.

The Eternal Son

Someone's thinking about his mother tonight.

The wakeful son
of a parent who hardly sleeps,

the sleepless father of his own
restless child, God, is it you?
Is it me? Do you have a mother?

Who mixes flour and sugar
for your birthday cake?

Who stirs slumber and remembrance
in a song for your bedtime?

If you're the cry enjoining dawn,
who birthed you?

If you're the bell tolling night
without circumference, who rocked you?

Someone's separating
the white grains of his insomnia
from the black seeds
of his sleep.

If it isn't you, God, it must be me.

My mother's eternal son,
I can't hear the rain without thinking
it's her in the next room
folding our clothes to lay inside a suitcase.

And now she's counting her money
on the bed, the good paper

and the paper from the other country
in separate heaps.

If day comes soon, she could buy our passage.
But if our lot is the rest of the night,
we'll have to trust unseen hands
to hand us toward ever deeper sleep.

Then I'll be the crumb
at the bottom of her pocket,
and she can keep me
or sow me on the water,
as she pleases. Anyway,

she has too much to carry, she who knows
night must tell the rest of every story.

Now she's wondering about the sea.
She can't tell if the white foam laughs
I was born dark! while it spins
opposite the momentum of our dying,

or do the waves journey beyond
the name of every country
and the changing color of her hair.

And if she's weeping,
it's because she's misplaced
both of our childhoods.

And if she's humming, it's because
she's heard the name of life:
A name, but no name, the dove

bereft of memory and finally singing
how the light happened
to one who gave up
ever looking back.

Fill and Fall

After crying, Child,
there's still singing to be done.

As long as night is one country
on both sides of our window,

as long as each of us remains a face
dreaming a face,

each must trace his heart's own steep path:
night and falling.

So sing your heart's first abandonment,
and measure the span
each falling thing endures.

Then sing the country under speech,
dark hillsides of an older singing
out-living
all of our fond names for God.

What does day proclaim there
where birds glean all of our remaindered shadow?
Stop crying, or you'll be late.

After wings
and the shadows of wings, there's still
the whole ungrasped body
of flying to uncover.

After standing, outnumbered, under petals
and their traceless falling

out of yesterday
and into open want,

we've still the fruit to meet,
still the ancient shapes
of jars and bowls to weigh,

and still the empty hands
in which the hours never pool.

For there's no place
my hand, full of its own
going away,
ever found along a body
falling beside me.

And the way to the crowning grapes lies sealed
to all but one who's heard
what nights are for: falling
and singing the fall,

as water falls, ringing,
to fill and fall, overwhelming
basin after basin.

As each must kneel
inside himself to find
the tiered slopes
only brimming masters.

Dwelling

As though touching her
might make him known to himself,

as though his hand moving
over her body might find who
he is, as though he lay inside her, a country

his hand's traveling uncovered,
as though such a country arose
continually up out of her
to meet his hand's setting forth and setting forth.

And the places on her body have no names.
And she is what's immense about the night.
And their clothes on the floor are arranged
for forgetfulness.

Restless

I can hear in your voice
you were born in one country
and will die in another.

And where you live is where you'll be buried,
and when you dream it's where you were born,

and the moon hangs in both skies
on the same night.

And that's why you think the moon has a sister.
That's why your day is hostage to your nights.

And that's why you can't sleep except by forgetting.
You can't love except by remembering.

And that's why you're divided: *Yes* and *No*.
I want to die. I want to live.
Never go away. Leave me alone.

I can hear by what you say
your first words must have been *mother* and *father*.

Even before your own name, *mother*.
Long before *amen*, *father*.

And when you lie down you tuck them
under your pillow, where they give rise
to other words: *childhood*, *fate*, and *rescue*.
Heaven, *wine*, *return*.

And even *god* and *death* are offspring.
Even world is begotten, even *summer*
a descendant. And the apple tree. Look

and see the entire
lineage, all the words, alive
in every leaf and branching
decision, snug
inside each fast bud,

all in every flower,
together inside the pulp, and mingling
in the fragrance
of the first taste and the last.

I can tell by your silence you've seen the petals
immense in their vanishing.

Flying, they build your only dwelling.
Falling, they sow shadows at your feet.

And when you close your eyes
you think you hear
the ancient fountains
from which they spring,

rock and water ceaselessly declaring
the laws of coming and going.

Out of Hiding

Someone said my name in the garden,

while I grew smaller
in the spreading shadow of the peonies,

grew larger by my absence to another,
grew older among the ants, ancient

under the opening heads of the flowers,
new to myself, and stranger.

When I heard my name again, it sounded far,
like the name of the child next door,
or a favorite cousin visiting for the summer,

while the quiet seemed my true name,
a near and inaudible singing
born of hidden ground.

Quiet to quiet, I called back.
And the birds declared my whereabouts all morning.

www.ingramcontent.com/pod-product-compliance
Ingram Content Group UK Ltd.
Pitfield, Milton Keynes, MK11 3LW, UK
UKHW041419180426
11947UKWH00007B/214